I0187688

plug; *outlet*

BACKLASH

PRESS

A pioneering publishing house dedicated to creating intelligent, vivid books. Established to inform, educate, entertain, and provoke.

A Backlash Press Book

First edition 2024

backlashpress.com

Poetry by A.M. Heffernan

ISBN: 978-1-0686972-7-2

All rights reserved. No part of this publication may be reproduced, stored in a retrieval system, or transmitted in any form or by any means, electronic, mechanical, photocopying, recording or otherwise, without permission of the copyright holder.

Copyright @ A.M. Heffernan
The moral rights of the author have been asserted.

plug; *outlet*

poetry by A.M. Heffernan

Backlash Poetry
American Dangerous: Renée Olander
Bombing the Thinker: Darren C. Demaree
Burial Machine: Jacob Griffin Hall
Clay Unbreakables: Natalia I Andrievskikh
Into The The: Robin Reagler
Phantom Laundry: Michael Tyrell
Tattered Scrolls and Postulates: Joseph V. Milford
The Arsonist's Letters: Michael Tyrell
Unfinished Murder Ballads: Darren C. Demaree
Some Things that have Happened so Far: Gareth Culshaw
Nobody, Nowhere, USA: Gret Heffernan

Backlash Journals
One, Two, Three, Four, Five, Isolation

Backlash Fiction and Nonfiction
The Sculptor: Gret Heffernan
Dark Ansley 01, 02: Gret Heffernan
Life in the Sky Falls Down: Bruce Bromley
The Sky Within: Rebecca Stonehill

Backlash publishes multiple zines, pamphlets, and printed material.

To Nana

1.

i spent the night trying to breathe on my own,
bound by red shoelaces and false ideologies, i was stuck by the
unrelenting force of a million tiny soldiers,
troops of pity and fear for myself circling my carcass like lions,
prey to the poor hearted.
trapped in that small red room,
my shoes coming undone.

2.

a thorn has jabbed me further into the palms of change,
my face is stroked by rose petals from the bush planted at my birth,
impaled at every moment of life,
every second of my being,
reminding me of the paradox of my small section of spotlight.
behind us are the pale sheer skins of the past,
shed off like a snake i crawl into my shiny new costume,
and face the crowd.

3.

goodnight you whispered,
your words held on your lip like a bird might clutch onto a dead branch,
my throat appeared parched and soundless.

goodnight, 9 letters escaping like bees from the hive of your mouth,
buzzing around me, i had no motivation to swat them away,
their stings would hold no harm.

"goodnight";
tears arose and grew absently,
i let them overwhelm my eyes.
they swarmed like wasps,
dangerous and in no way understandable,
i was unable to swat them away.
i felt the clutch of your blue fingers.

goodnight,
9, 18, 27,
over, forte, a crescendo of noise,
helpless you choked.
hold on screamed the widening of my eyes;
my words may be able to replace the ocean but could never be large
enough to fill your absence.
winter had hushed your hive,
your hum stopped and laid dormant,
embraced by soiled life.

goodnight i questioned,
careful, deliberate,

my knees dirty,
my heart soiled.
no response ailed my illness,
your clutch no longer existed,
your everything had been replaced by granite,
coldly, the grave held no love,
yet you still live on through moments of glow.

goodnight was my final whisper,
my skin illuminated by the roundness of your face,
goodnight moon.

4.

i'm dying to meet you moon face,
face of razor light.
maybe one day, once my hands are laid eternally by my sides,
and my skin resembles chlorinated water,
and my life has sent me back into the womb,
wounded me into a sleep so peaceful my everything will exist only
behind orange lighting and crescent teacups,
we shall exchange whispers through messy hair and unwashed faces,
and i might remember your name the way i once did,
i wish to know you moon face,
dance with me through the musk of bluebell light,
guide me through waters and lay me under you,
shower me with glares,
let me remember you moon face,
for your face was once familiar,
your lips exist only in the black of my pupils,
glow greetings onto me,
i wish to meet you moon face.

5.

little faces appearing under the lazy haze of glowing sun,
rested like a pearl between the strings of a child's amateur
harpsichord,
played soft and low,
shy, afraid of a too much or too little pitch,
sat listening under bows of orange flowers and lemons,
smelling citrus,
inhaling joy,
boiling away the cold hard brew of wet sat still and dormant in the
pit of an old, old stomach.

6.

tiny angels of silver drift back to the stars,
north of the moon,
lick salt off the chin of a crescent rock,
and glow inside of little pearly handprints like a single orange light
in the big black ocean.

7.

weights hanging like loose strings off a golden heart,
fraying with resentment, fear,
sweat forming beads on the forehead of your child as she walks
backward slowly,
retreating from a chase she can't win,
red the monster, blue the child,
woman of purple will break the ribbon,
and she will disappear,
flipped into her pupil,
sprinting back to the soft comfort of black.

8.

pour stars into my void,
fill me and pick at me like crows to meat,
starve me, and listen to droplets twinkle under the sun.
string me up like a guitar,
and listen to me play melodies sad enough for the ocean to pour out
of your eyes,
complete me,
end me whole,
supernova me into an abyss as deep and as concave as your eyes,
black holes,
i fall.

9.

opposite thought:
parallel index
wondering,
repeating to yourself the same speech over and over and over just
longing, waiting, watching love surround you,
still unable to touch you.
become a part of the set crew in your own life and feel painfully
aware of the loneliness you feel whilst around others.
bottle your feelings and send them off in painted bottles of blue and
black,
watch them float, gasp, and drown like your momentum,
have a staring contest with your own reflection and pay the cost of
your sanity.

10.

moth wings beat like guitar strings,
backwards velvet up spinal cords,
a foolish framed fucker,
existing between every pucker in every line of a diary,
muck, mucky, unclean,
wash, scrub scream your work off of my hands,
or slice the bugs out of my skin,
stop the crawl,
stop all the brawling and clawing and flaunting of your control,
helpless,
hopeless and stuck like a cup half filled,
help me control the darkness overload,
help me muffle the screams,
before i turn into the monster under the bed,
before you have read and stroked and killed my dreams, cold, dead.

11.

i lay, dark; small,
surrounded, shrouded by my big, big enigma,
their hands grope my throat,
eyes mask my vision with dark.
follow me,
lead me to the dark,
shake me and hold my breath as if i never had breathed,
as if my lungs were desert land and veins were green,
lull me in lukewarm water and bathe away my problems until i exist
in a white room,
wipe condensation from my glasses,
and curl around me like a shell over a snail,
stoop and sting me with our tears,
help me to create an ocean.

12.

head against the mirror;
pink and purple dancers weaving in and out of sight,
wheeze like a horse till your breath is as small as a lizard and you are
curled up like a conch shell,
whisper, very slowly your beliefs into my ears and decorate them
with little red bows and blue sparkles,
and drift in a red jacket away from my eyelids,
drift in red,
slow, soft, conserved.

13.

i wish that i were bulletproof so that even stars could not pierce me,
skin made of chainmail and eyes the colour of steel,
bulletproof and under Texas sun,
in love with the green of limes or the brushstrokes of cranes in the
sky on top of me,
bulletproof enough to be able to enjoy beauty,
bulletproof to erase fear like the morning erases night,
around to surpass others,
to be alone,
alone or safe?
chainmail channelling loneliness,
ask a soldier,
chainmail only acts as a weight on your shoulders.

14.

take me away,
far, far away from the terrors that await me,
check the bed,
check for monsters;
check for a life unlived,
and old age unloved,
stray berries stain skin and seep from cuts deep and personal.
scars,
a chance to revive the past,
a way around time,
hair; much the same as scars,
root to tip, not tip to root,
young to old, not old to young,
an inevitable countdown to death,
is the only thing we know life is for.

15.

how does it feel to bully yourself?
how does a word smash into fragmented insecurities?
unravelled thread:
undone by the worn hands of women hood,
what does it mean to be a woman?
to have your own thread woven by men?
or to undo their mistakes and replace it with gold string,
to stitch dreams and embezzle pain into your string,
until it's fleshy and human,
real and tarnished like an old fireplace,
until what you have created is not a piece of string,
it's yourself in a smashed mirror,
to gape back at you,
to remember is to be a woman.

16.

you look at me and glisten rays onto my face, aware of the fact that
you were told to stay secret,
hidden from my eyes,
yet here you are,
euphoric, purple beauty gleaming from the sky of suns,
otherworldly,
human,
roots through you travel through all our eyes,
connecting us all on a thin, clear string like cranberries on a
Christmas garland,
or paper chains made by children,
inevitably, we are all the same.

17.

as you obtain your own demise in fragmented pieces of flesh,
or rise into your eyelids through your own artificial daydreams,
you suicidally turn on lights in a house you had no idea people could
see into.

18.

dancing in your arms in the night of suns,
stillness slides under our fingertips through what felt like everything,
apocalyptic change,
your shift from north to south grabbing my secret naivety like
questions grasp the mind of a child,
why do your eyes show peril,
where did the love go,
running through what i thought was our blood,
the blood on your fingers was not your own,
it was red, like mine,
not your black inhumane carrier of life,
the blood on your fingertips,
once danced with mine like those little beautiful tulips danced with
the grass on that night we thought it was just us,
and now i find myself holding my own arm,
staring into your eyes as you,
the other woman,
grin from above,
your hands stippling streams of whiskey life into my eyes and ears,
making me die again.

19.

pale lipped and wonky teethed she smiles,
her gums revealed in the lipstick stained mirror,
painfully she plucks radiance out of a face once wet with baby tears,
painted scars crease her eye bags,
and as the pack disappears like floating tortured angels over the
silver blue mountain,
the salt of another child nourishes her face,
and in that same mirror,
lipstick stained and dusty as always,
the same unperfected grin grips her lungs,
and squeezes her irises,
until gradually she's surrounded by black horses and light green
sugared skies,
and she's a bird once again,
awaiting the day that cage doors rust over and release her from her
bondage,
and she's as small as a pocket poppet,
young enough to connect with the sea,
and pure enough to leave the world,
into the pomegranate purple sun,
and away to sleep on the surface of the moon.

20.

the song of your face makes my bare soul ache with intense rolls of
pain and beauty,
pure, bloody, uncaring emotion,
your wrapped up love in folds of letters pages and pen man ship of
swirly ink,
your eyes connected with mine in a knot of love, of life, of all
importance,
of all beauty,
and your pain hits like dreams in heaven,
like deep sleep in hell,
like blood in cracks,
like paint in cuts,
like your eyes blood shot red.

21.

how open i feel,
as my womanhood bursts budding light through bark and lilac skies,
as my hair drifts along secluded streams whispering secrets into only
my own ears,
perfect harmonies joined with the black and blues of the peace i find
in watching my trees dance to the rhythm of the wind,
what beauty i pump through my chest,
as i see stars above and clasp lockets and little wisps of glitter to my
cheeks in simple joy,
as i watch little girls cling onto my hands and grip my fingers tight as
we explore our vibrant nature,
and what peace i feel,
as my moon glimpses at me through reflections on my window sill,
as all of my little girls life and light and laugh and heart,
lay drowsy in the pits of my mind and soul,
kept safe in a locket; my love.

22.

Claire is the only one living you on,
her soft fingers beating out the rhythms of your lost life,
your riffs of emotion,
and as you dance between my eyes in bathroom mirrors and bed
sheets,
she mimics your touch through unseen billows,
and here you are again,
in the purple piano's arms,
tiptoeing in the sky.

23.

school girl loves you like a mirror loves a pretty pocket,
the lights dim within her tartan vessel,
purple eruptions in eyes filled with emotion deeper than the black of
the empty solar system,
deeper than the well i dropped my wish for you in,
purple eruptions everywhere.

24.

a child's eyes returned to slumber,
burdened by a single salty droplet on its decent down fresh fleshy
cheeks,
she wished upon a whale once,
it's skin speckled by blue water,
and it's eyes glassy from all it had seen,
washed upon sandy beaches
her wish stuck on like a limpet,
her dreams crushed under silky pale skin.
her face was a picture of crows,
as shrill as fox cries,
her mind getting used to this feeling,
lingered disappointed throughout her skin,
her bones

25.

neck clicked backwards against the bed of a dark wooden bedpost,
a girls fine features drawn in with graphite lines lay, alone.
her hair is penetrated by dust as time whirls around her,
her face moves just enough for her to be alive,
i love them more than anything,
i wonder if they feel the same
splattered obnoxious noise.

26.

aching.
aching slowly through crusted marron bones,
through my clutched heart, beating within its cage,
unsymmetrical faces underneath pressured air deforms into perfect souls,
dog eyes grimace with pain of elderly responsibility,
like a may fly might feel for it's one day of life,
underlyingly imperfect within their silk,
rotten robes.

27.

i catch the glimpse of your eye softening in the string quartets of true sky;
the colours of fire and light rising as the sun falls,
i'm brushed by you when you move the leaves under my feet,
i'm seen by you through a glass shield of blue ocean,
never leave me,
and i will always see you in the moon,
planets apart,
wings preventing us from holding each other again,
in the wind,
the forces of nature,
i'll always see you.

28.

cracked open empty shells of what your life was,
what your life used to be,
empty duck eggs speckled with blue rain and searing pain,
i crunch along your broken path,
searching for your glass eyes,
your China cheeks,
your pale blue lines under thin skin,
the warmth of angry red that spoke words of life and memories,
your face was illuminated by our human gift,
when you were plucked away from our lives,
you were as peaceful as a humming bird clutched within delicate
lavender buds,
you were as ready as a desert is for water,
i was as ready as fish is for land,
you left at your end,
you left at my beginning,
i'll end with you,
just as i started,
i'll see you in the moon.

29.

inside of my plagued mind,
i sit, sprawled out like a teddy bear on a floor of dynamite,
blown up bodies around me,
restless hair atop my head of widened soldiers eyes,
red dances waltz around my only private room,
spinning me around and around,
yearning, crying for my love,
as i use its hands to tear into souls of blue,
opposites don't attract,
they destroy each other.

30.

and in the lines of the fingerprint of the universe,
you were sucked under,
my head floating in a paddling pool of spinning dirty water as we
giggled and swam in circles,
curled in on itself like a dandelion,
lumpy throated,
teary eyed,
but i still feel nothing.
i still feel nothing but
but nothing.

31.

greedy malevolent undertaker of uncertain memories,
wanting, craving more as i whisk away uncertain truths obscured by
thoughts purple haze,
unfinished years with people whose lives add a few more pages into
family albums covered with dust and secrets never to be revealed,
laying underground in our minds as beds for coffins,
solid oak and unneeded cushioned padding surfacing our hollowed,
angry lives,
more was needed,
i and you shall be unwholly together for eternity, and exist the same
in each other's minds.

32.

when you are like a cup filled with gazed eyes and masks with lips
that don't speak and lids that don't close,
a refill may be needed,
to hang your face on the wall and stare at it with your clean slate that
was once found beautiful,
before you glue it back on,
and once again face masks made by hands better than your own.

33.

will you leave the light on if i try and find you,
maybe not as no one's home,
maybe one day,
when leaves have scattered and claimed the most precious bits of
your four cornered rooms,
we could hold each other's hands tight,
breathe deeply, and put one foot in front of the other to Grace our
past,
or maybe we could just love each other as big as the moon.

34.

i watch her sneer back at me in the windshield of a very loud car,
her whispering voices sounding like lilac in my mind;
unbalanced to the motion of life,
her comfort coming from a place of bitter icy wind and nothingness,
her grimy nails isolating my skin from my organs as it peels back my
heart like a piece of soggy paper stuck to a piece of tile.
her language analysed by characters grasping her shoulders,
it's too late.
her voice gets louder as the floor rises and life falls through gaps in
crooked floorboards,
slipped from the strong grasp of weight over years and years, over
eras and periods of time lost to others,
her voice gets louder as i lose you,
as you get tugged away from me,
and no matter how well i hold you, how well i anchor my legs,
no amount of heavy ships could help you not sail away from me,
over the horizon,
away, away, away.

35.

i wake up, breathless in a pool of red hot blood.
my blood.
my blood made from my body,
and yet it's not mine really.
it's on the hands of another.
trapped inside of my mattress banging and thrashing in the tight
sheets until it can rip through the layer like a curtain.
until it can rip its way out of me, and make me bleed red hot blood.
not my blood.

36.

blood oozes out of the hatred machine.
oh ugly red hatred machine,
how you make me loathe,
how you make my shirt sheer with torrential tears,
how you expose more than what is seen,
how you make me want to hurt,
to feel pain.
oh ugly red hatred machine,
your ruby dribbles drip,
to feel your love is to be almost, almost dead.
to be alive is to be pretty when you cry. fuck that.

37.

your power is appreciated by the humour of your senseless worship,
and your face is appreciated by people you don't know,
men, whose jutting, deformed personalities run deep and darkly into
their eyes and their lips,
but i do not appreciate your power,
or you need for it,
or your display of false identity and fake love,
you live as if you do not feel,
or cannot feel,
you live as if you are a simple no good rock, how i wish i could kick
you aimlessly along the pavement.
and yet,
your eyes close every night,
and you pupils dilate with the morning sun,
and you never think that i might be the one who has to discover the
core of your identity,
the pulpy bloody mess that is left unnoticed in the small room that is
yourself,
and you feel no shame,
none at all.

38.

a girl once nestled into the comforting arms of her stripy linen
bedsheets,
for once her smile lines were gone,
and her hair was framing her face nicely,
however she sobbed into the arms of her trusted space,
which rocked her back and forth
like the child she used to be,
her lungs were full with air yet she needed more,
caressed by a blade,
and wrenched in the gut,
confided with erotomania and heartache,
her mind felt as if a snake had soaked hot poison over her thoughts,
and in the silence of her room,
and the thundering booms of the quiet,
she was perfectly, brilliantly human,
and no more.

39.

heart ached like opposite magnets,
eyes contaminated with lakes of unwanted fiercely salty water.
all she wanted was to fly like those big glorious pink flamingos.

40.

how much time has passed by my baby bassinet,
cradled shook mind,
when did the line in the sky turn from blue to orange to grey to
black,
when did the light leech its way on,
when did it happen,
time and time again i call my inner telephone,
asking,
asking,
asking,
i'm on hold.
suspended like an aeroplane taking off.
i am suspended,
parallel to my answers.

41.

i stare at the mirror,
the window,
the glass,
until the reflection is unrecognisable by my eyes,
are they green or blue?
she's not me,
i have no idea who i am anymore,
it's like i'm living a life,
balancing on the top of a thin page of a long, long book,
if only i could fall back into my story,
because i have no idea where i'm going.

42.

an old, old women bore the hands of a bare, bare baby,
it's eyes ethereally glossy,
open, just,
its hands grasping like soft ferns;
brushing, tickling mothers worn, dimpled neck.
mother sweet,
mother gentle,
mother may only love the plum purple wisteria that she birthed,
like a big, naked, blooming, beautiful sky,
round,
endless.

43.

rocks feel soft under feet hardened by the blue lagoons refreshing and
nurturing waters,
and the sweetest of birds,
a blue tits cry misunderstood by a baby's young and bloody ears,
shrill wails fall from earthy soiled ground,
quiet, and desperate as a bee for its pollen,
lilac map routs through water weave and develop as a road for fish,
ever moving and ever flowing,
accustomed to changing due to the seas indecisive mood,
and in the silent of the morning,
the only thing awake:
the jolting lizards,
whisper their secrets to your sleeping, peaceful eyes.

44.

milky cat licked clouds,
mediterranean trees,
dead appearance signifies summer,
a yearn for skin to prove your sun exposure,
and hands,
sticky and wet from the squelching of peaches and plumbs,
child eyes giving sight to the ants,
fat and itchy.
mirrors that show the cold winter,
and lines that sink your soul into a despair.
all this into a mish mash of things,
pushed together like the opposite sides of magnets,
into one final combination,
of light and long days and blue,
deep, high, beautiful blue.

45.

rings of fingerprints,
just like ripples of water,
undone by string pulled through holes,
carrying age and carrying responsibility,
cranes fly,
and i die,
i miss the freedom of being big and white and beautiful,
of drifting like a stray petal through the air,
now i am heavy and weighted by strong bones,
designed to resist the inevitable pain of age,
but not destined to repent it.

46.

a man sits alone on a hill,
it's colour is formed from a sky of green follicles,
and sadly he sits,
his back the shape of a deformed twig,
his hair in grey clay-like lines down his face,
a character of stop motion.
his sadness has finally pushed out of his heart,
it has enveloped him,
a symphony of strings play in his mind,
and pain,
pain is everywhere,
so he lays,
and breathes,
and exists,
all of him tortured,
sitting.

47.

bumping beats down the scale of music,
comfortably familiar,
yet completely new,
child eyes stare through a glass like hole,
they capture memories in unsettling truths or familiarity,
pictures caught on the line of life and marked with a bright red pin,
i wonder when the light flickered off.

48.

silent truths being lied about by silent lies,
uncovered snips of emotion judged and marvelled over by people
that know your current numb and empty state.
i give you happiness, she said,
rarely felt by those who consciously wait for it.
i want to go back to the time when people didn't wish it was the past,
i wonder if a time ever existed;
where people know the outcome of their future.
mud covered hands are only learning how to dig away the surface of
my life,
yet sometimes,
i feel utterly like i have lived enough,
still a child,
yet consumed by adulthood,
i'm not ready,
bring me back.

49.

i wish you had stayed with me,
led me through life telling me that childhood will be missed,
looked to the future to foreshadow the sadness that clutches me.
given me a chance to go back,
when the sky gifted a colour to the blue so beautiful that happiness
arose onto any sole beneath it,
and when life sounded as perfect as the popping of a bubble,
or the chirp of a cricket.
i wish i was free again,
that the cranking rusty cogs of my life were once again freshly oiled,
new and perfect.
that life was good once more,
where has it all gone,
please come back to me,
bring me my life back.

50.

solitude hours stuck in sticky unresolved silence through tears
plopping onto hard ripe flesh.
my end state being not only my finish,
but my perishing position.
my back braced in fear for the future that may happen.
i wait,
my silence might astound those who see me wrong.
reality is not a thing here.
i'm stuck,
my arms are tired from banging on glass windows to get out into the
world,
so they sink into the floor,
given up.
my light has flickered out from a whisper of a child once known as
myself,
she wants her mind back.

51.

dark green haze,
trees almost colourless in the dying sun,
giving up its light for another day.
peaceful, unreluctantly calm,
a tranquillity that comes from sadness,
anguish of thoughts beyond your comprehension,
i'm stuck in a dark green haze.

52.

sparks of happiness unknown and foreign to my current soul,
vast winter nights tufted over like the flick of a hummingbird's wing,
people suddenly joyous at the sight of something that has always
been there,
a torch of the skies,
beaming lines of light into the eyes of the unexpected,
its return awaited,
its arrival lingered,
she's finally here.

53.

hide underneath that blanket dear girl,
hide your sorrow,
for salt should come from the sea,
and darkness should come from a lacking of light,
no one is looking for you,
but you are guilty for passing a fluttered eye while searching for
them,
the shame is great,
we all suffer, yours is just physical,
my physical suffering,
the endurance of great moving lines,
massive, magnificent bugs,
scuttling over my body,
their stomachs lurching great fat breaths of moist mud,
trampling truly impressive feats of dejection over my empty skull,
shame.

54.

light and dark green melted into the terracotta red earth,
and whispers of bug life coincides
peacefully with the fragile birds landing on white washed rooftops
and carefully layered tiles,
empty peach juice bottles laying around half melted glasses of ice,
and slowly sipping wasps,
their wings reflected by the bright tangerine light.
all a perfect array of colours juxtaposed by an obnoxious table cloth
with chipping, rusty chairs.
thighs exposed,
half shaved and sloping elegantly under tables,
with shorts, rolled and sticky from the heat.
under the soft sun comes an intense, sludgy heat that seems to be
repelled by the slow moving branches of trees stretching,
taking the form of barriers over dazed people,
a complete sense of relaxation washed over them as dappled sunlight
moves wistfully over their dark bodies and wavy hair.
a perfect summer day to be followed by another.

55.

love takes time,
the green man states,
throwing the burden of these words out into the air like a ball,
or a flicked bug.
not acknowledging the weight it holds,
of course he would say that,
only the green man would say that.
maybe the orange man or the pink man would say the words,
love takes time,
with softly blinking eyes,
and a hard dusty focus inhabiting his solemn face,
or with a careful stare into the eyes of another,
a moment soon forgotten,
but left to sit quiet as other memories chatter loudly,
sitting at the back of your head so that maybe one day,
you will take comfort in those words,
take comfort in solitude,
the green man would never do that.

56.

and as the daffodils began to rise,
her mascara was picked off with desperate fingers,
and her clothes pulled away to reveal a body that she thought needed
work but didn't at all.
her hair was more wild,
and her eyes grew from mirroring death,
to reflecting life.
and as trees were blossoming the music began to slow,
and all of those things,
the missing things of the past,
arose from the crevices of her bedroom,
clothes from before were found,
and her sense of life was being relinquished,
her feeling of resistance to death was increased,
and all was better,
not great,
but better,
she was okay,
and that's all that mattered,
she is okay.
now repeat that sentence again.

57.

a rising child of unfathomable beauty beyond the molecules that
make her,
just standing is a privilege,
for her sun skin,
and moon eyes reflect the starting sky as she looks for advice,
space child.

and as she gazed,
love flourished as dancing rings in her eyes,
falling as she stared
into eyes the same as hers,
a hole to the mind,
letting each other enter,
reach the internal position of your mind,
the need to possess you as their own.

58.

just like a lip touch or a hand hold,
i would give all of myself to them.
stay endlessly joined by the emotional unbalance i feel.
fold myself into them to make them a shell protecting me.
the potter works the clay,
finger lines and prints of original indentations forming our faces,
melded together,
we are one,
a solar system dependant.

59.

billows of blue sea tasting droplets drip, drip dripping down tiny
veins of irregular tunnels through skin.
fleeing from unwelcome feelings and distant songs.
making your music filled ears burn with desire of premium happiness,
a foxes life to the price of nothing.
the sun should inject itself into my skin through radiations of bright
light,
filling this girls mouth with soft,
pure ease,
but instead,
my skin is filled with mirrors,
reflecting the light,
i feel like the depths of the ocean,
dark and tired.
my skin is indented with blue,
purple and black,
others is a beautiful orange or perfect yellow,
i'm jealous of their complexions of perfect sun,
sun kissed children.

60.

and as she looked through the world through her soft eyes,
they hardened with the realisation that nothing is right,
and suddenly she needed to fix all,
she called it her duty,
it's my 'privilege' she spoke,
her eyes once soft of greenish hue now turned blue,
piercing and horrible,
like the seas reflected by the light of the moon,
deep and rippling,
angry.
this was not my purpose, but now i suppose it is, she recalled,
for her life is different now,
her grasp on yellow sunlight has slipped,
and now she holds her eyes,
they are dripping with retching red rubies,
falling to the ground and bouncing into one another as if they were
never precious at all,
she pulled out her own eyes,
scratched them from her scalp until she was ugly and deformed,
she is not the way she wanted to be,
but put it upon herself,
for it was her fingers that dug out the indented,
greenish hue,
once her eyes.

61.

the flies,
wobbly on their axes of floating sunlight,
up then down,
circling in a whirlwind of rich light through circles of orange and
light pinky red,
drifting around one another,
like drunk,
dim ants,
they have lost their way in the line.

62.

my world,
my world would be wonderful and woeful,
my world,
my world would be different and uncomplicated,
in my world,
bluebells would smell like roses,
and roses would smell like daffodils,
because bluebells are better than roses,
in my world,
trees would be orange, and grass would be purple,
but the sky would stay blue, because the sky is perfect.
in my world,
leaves would fall in spring,
and would flourish in winter like a warm blanket around the tree.
but in this world,
bluebells are purple,
and roses smell like roses,
in this world,
the grass and trees clash in colour of green and green,
in this world,
trees are cold in winter,
and too hot in summer.
in this world,
things are beautifully perfect.

63.

a spider spins it's web with deafening care,
an individual, unnoticed care only to be rained on and made more
beautiful,
the rain makes it special,
not the spider,
the spider is the carer for the home,
the intricacies of the web made by herself,
held by other sources,
thin, unstable,
like an orbit,
the sun casts its light on things to make it seen,
to make a faint glow appear and produce a beautiful and perfect
preference,
undeniably special,
undeniably perfect.

64.

one cold hand grasped the other,
as the evil laugh spurts forcefully out of the monsters mouth,
the bright lights upon her crouched silhouette,
it stares her into the eyes,
green filled with chuckles of no remorse,
suddenly a beat music jumps into her ears,
hopping quickly upon her senses,
sprinting from one object of grief to the other,
perplexing her emotions,
and making her feel numb,
motionless,
dead.

65.

the crumpled mashed knees of life,
bowing to time,
it's one true nemesis,
might as-well enjoy those oceans of blue,
you don't know when you are going to fall,
unable to stand and support any longer,
so you fall,
arms outstretched,
no one will grasp them with passionate appreciation for the impact
of your life,
so enjoy the oceans of blue god dammit.

66.

she sat,
sitting at the bottom of the stairs,
her silk dress making a puddle around her bare feet,
she had covered it with her robe,
a stark contrast between textures that felt strange on her skin,
her hair a tangled mess,
tucked behind her ears,
she picked at the stiff mascara sticking to her eyes,
tugging out her lashes while doing so,
she let out a pent up persistent sigh
her breath heavy with the words she had spoken that day,
and with her thoughts she sat,
sitting at the bottom of the stairs.

67.

and slowly their face turns white and pale in your mind,
and you only see them for the good,
the pure, the honest,
for you,
they are the angel faced memory,
chipped out of the past.

68.

lonely is that bench,
not even the shrivelled sad old man can keep it company,
it is imprisoned to not move,
the sea is its cinema,
every morning,
the sky awakes to a new hue of yellow,
and every morning that bench awakes with it,
the south waters drifting by,
the gulls showing off their freedom by swooping down and up,
every evening,
the sky drifts away,
that benches big yellow friend waves goodbye,
and all is lost for another day,
and the bench is lonely once again.

69.

i grip the ditch wall,
my sweaty hands are tough and thick skinned,
they somehow are being sliced,
torn and butchered,
a hand comes clean off the slippery edge,
a cry slips from my mouth as my body dangles like a slab of fresh
meat;
ready to be devoured,
suspended to hang dry.

70.

a water girl.
not being dragged, but dragging herself,
slowly softly slivering into the slushing sunset,
her face radiated by clear reflections,
a deep musty peace,
open and free,
her feet slowly scraping nothing,
she is unaware that she is falling,
or that the sun is lowering,
she embraces the darkness,
holds it tight as it wraps her in its calm,
just like a mother may hold her child,
with terrifying love,
and terrifying potential,
yet the child will still trust.
a water girl.

71.

it stuck with me like an ugly, sticky, fluorescent orange plaster,
noticeable and sickening,
i will noticeably remember that comment,
it shall be known as a time of hurt and anger,
i may have a lot of plasters,
my face is covered,
my arms, my legs,
we should all remember the concept of plasters,
they heal the wound,
they cover it,
making it more noticeable until it's gone,
there will be a time of no more ugly orange plasters,
there will.

72.

a mango sky,
a vibrato of creamy orange,
yellow and lilac,
surfacing over the tedious clouds,
someday,
i would like to go to there,
become a gull and drift dreamily dancing across the clouds,
my feathers of dull drastically replaced,
the rippling reflection across my glossy wings,
suddenly a new, vibrant colour of the delicate, delicious dying sun.
i may swoop at my will,
between the untouched clouds,
and the golden rays.
my fingertips sliding, smoothly,
flush against winged tips.
some day.

73.

on the brink of figuring it out,
tip me over the edge,
just enough,
for a quick fall,
before another surface bashes and crashes underneath me.

74.

screaming as my mind snarls it's ugly face,
the shock of it is enough to startle,
they dig deeper,
crunching through the barriers,
splintering the cartilage,
until i am there with a murderous mind,
it has hurt me,
i am bleeding out,
spluttering and breathless,
it's an overload,
stuck.

75.

her wide eyes deceive her,
she falls down,
leaving only her spirit as a virtue to what she was before she knew
this life was unkind,
a sacrifice for the chosen,
a bare lifeless body,
picked and torn,
a lonely spluttering heart,
gashes and stains,
the carpet is red now,
and she is resurfacing,
entering herself again with bitter realisation,
"what is opened cannot be closed."

76.

a child,
born of the sun,
her iridescent skin and gemstone eyes,
yet she is raised by the moon,
it's icy core digging deep into her soul,
engulfing her with darkness,
a beautiful,
serene darkness,
inching its way into every forgotten corner,
every glimmer of the eye,
this child is the mistake between two worlds,
to planets
she is believed to be somewhat of the imagination,
like a number,
it's not really there.

77.

the quiet of the green,
it fills me with suspense,
surrounded with memories,
the past engraved softly with swirling patterns through the dense,
tough shield,
they are watching, swaying with the breath of a thousand beetles and
birds,
a force of nature,
others dependant on its wellbeing,
it is constantly chipping away,
it's leaves,
swiftly falling onto the rich ground of decaying matter,
what does it mean to be a tree,
does it harness the light from the sun, to draw it closer to the earth
so that it may bathe in the light of a million fires,
does it continue on its cycle to achieve an unknown treasure,
every year the cranes fly over them, flapping their sleek, bony wings,
does it long to feel those feathers, to experience their soft, weightless
touch upon its impenetrable limbs, it knows the force it could show
on a creature unseizable to its sheer mass and weight,
they are distant creatures, they listen to rumble of conversations,
silently joining in,
appreciative of the company,
one may always go back to the trees,
for they have heard it all,
they shall listen.

78.

a phrase unknown to my prior self:
a heavy heart,
a personal understanding of something that I realise is not a phrase
at all,
but rather a statement of truth,
a heart weighed down by sadness and anxiety,
the palpitations gained from the never ending beat,
the walk of thirst and deprivation of your idealistic self,
a heart with a bag of solid loneliness sitting happily on its back,
never satisfied,
never completed,
until,
eventually,
the greedy crows peck away at its soul,
until its old being can't even recognise its future self,
until it's nothing,
that's when it gives up.

79.

a treacherous feeling of agony,
it escapes,
it fumbled through my heart,
its blindness makes it unaware of the pain it's committing,
it feels for the goodness,
the innocence,
the little things,
they are magnified until they blur my vision,
they cease to decrease in magnitude,
they stay,
shattering the strands of brilliance,
dimming the lights,
until it's all dark.

80.

the uncertainty that the crow will fall,
the whisps of encapsulated black,
slithering slowly onto the layer beneath,
drowning in the nothing around it,
the tip touches first,
then encases the darkness around the figure.

81.

all white flags up,
up to the pain,
up to the stress of my current state,
it's an undeniable feeling,
i surrender to my mind,
i surrender.

82.

when life breathes into my lungs,
a sweet release of pressure mixed with a powerful sense of childhood,
it bounces and trips around inside of me,
dancing to an always pulsating rhythm.

83.

i hear the voice,
defeating me,
my bruised eyes see the form in front of me,
staring back with those wide eyes,
my reflection bending and shaping,
i do not see myself,
i see an orb of regret and a weak rule follower,
i do not see a fighter,
i see nothing.

84.

we glide on the wings of ace's divine fear,
obsessing over the thin and unreliable heartbeat of life,
surviving on dishes of betrayal and hate,
scoffing down sorrowful days like a prisoner with clean water,
deafening the sound of voices with blood flowing to your ears,
hiding and dragging away from the memories hidden in the
undergrowth of your mind,
clawing and screeching up the mountainous climb to reach
confidence,
pushing and tugging at the scalps of others to reach who you want
to be.

85.

a body,
the same as a painting,
changing constantly by unknown hands,
unaware of the creation that it shall find at the end,
always moving in sync with the brush that shall softly wipe a wrinkle
or a crease,
slowly yet with purpose,
bending and developing each and every line.

86.

dried carcasses of memories lying on the floor,
time eating them away,
left in your labyrinth of thoughts.
by the end there is no way out,
you can only sit,
with yourself,
and your mind,
alone,
surrounded by the death of your past.

www.ingramcontent.com/pod-product-compliance
Lightning Source LLC
Chambersburg PA
CBHW021843090426
42811CB00033B/2121/J